To My Amazing Daughter

A Creative Way
to Calm the Spirit
and Soothe the Soul

Marci

Blue Mountain Press™
Boulder, Colorado

Copyright © 2017 by Marci.

All rights reserved. No part of this publication may be reproduced, stored in a retrieval system or transmitted in any form or by any means, electronic, mechanical, photocopying, recording or otherwise, without the written permission of the publisher.

ISBN: 978-1-68088-179-0

Children of the Inner Light is a registered trademark. Used under license.
Certain trademarks are used under license.

Printed in China.
First Printing: 2017

Blue Mountain Arts, Inc.
P.O. Box 4549, Boulder, Colorado 80306

Introduction

This delightful coloring book, designed especially for daughters, invites you to take a little time for yourself and tap into your creative side. As you move from one coloring page to the next, you'll be inspired by Marci's heartfelt messages that capture the unique feelings a parent has for a daughter while also being reminded of what is truly important in life. Marci's words will lead you to feel more connected with yourself and your family, as well as with the world around you. And the focused concentration that occurs when you color may bring unexpected solutions to the challenges of everyday living, as well as the sense of peace we all wish for in our lives, especially in today's hectic, busy times.

Marci created her trademark Children of the Inner Light® characters in black and white because she believes that we are so much more than physical beings and that the inner spirit knows no race or color. She hopes you will take her drawings and make them your own by using the tools and colors that best fit your personality and preferences. Here you can unplug, relax, and go to that place inside where your deepest thoughts and feelings reside. It is the same beautiful place that Marci visits each time she is moved to draw or write. This is the gift Marci wants to share with you as you make her lovable characters uniquely yours.

Happy Coloring!

When I think about you and how you've grown, I feel so proud. It's not just the beauty in your face... but your shining spirit that lights up my world! I don't know where the time has gone... or when yesterday became today... but each time I think of the joy you are in my life, all that comes to mind is "you're amazing!"

Wasn't it yesterday that you were a baby in my arms? I looked at your precious face and wondered where life would take you. Today, I look at the person you've become... strong, kind, thoughtful, caring, and optimistic... and I realize that the dreams I held in my heart for you have come true.

A daughter is a gift of hopes and wishes wrapped up in a beautiful life.

A daughter is an opportunity to reflect upon the past and a chance to see possibilities fulfilled.

A daughter is understanding, kind, compassionate, caring, and giving.

A daughter reminds you of how much you are loved.

A daughter's love remains forever in your heart.

10 Simple Things to Remember

1. Love is why we are here.

2. The most important day is today.

3. If you always do your best, you will not have regrets.

4. In spite of your best efforts, some things are just out of your control.

5. Things will always look better tomorrow.

6. Sometimes a wrong turn will bring you to exactly the right place.

7. Sometimes when you think the answer is "no," it is just "not yet."

8. True friends share your joy, see the best in you, and support you through your challenges.

9. God and your parents will always love you.

10. For all your accomplishments, nothing will bring you more happiness than the love you find.

Live your beliefs... and be a powerful example of love in the world.

Be compassionate... Life is difficult, and people are often working through private battles.

Demonstrate acts of kindness... "Little ones" are watching you and learning about compassion.

Encourage someone today... The words "everything will be okay" can lighten the heart of another. Share love... there is an endless supply.

Be hopeful... Your attitude will uplift the spirit of another.

Sometimes we feel that we are all alone, as life brings us challenges to overcome and hardships to bear. But when we least expect it, help can appear. It may be a kind word from a stranger or a phone call at just the right time, and we are suddenly surrounded with the loving grace of God. Miracles happen every day because angels are everywhere.

When you need encouragement, remember these things:

You are stronger than you realize.

Life's inevitable adversities call forth our courage.

You have a lot of wisdom inside you.

God's plan will unfold with perfect timing.

The voice of your soul will lead the way.

A hug from my heart is only a phone call away!

So often we wonder about the "whys" in life... "Why did this happen?" "Why me?" "Why now?" But there is a secret that wise people know... Bumps in the road are an inevitable part of life that soften us, make us grow, and bestow upon us the virtue of compassion. Often it is only with the passing of time that it becomes clear that the cloud really did have a silver lining, and now we have wisdom, strength, and hope to share. And at last, we understand the true meaning of the phrase "Everything happens for a reason."

Listen for that voice inside guiding you toward the right thing to do, the right path to travel, and the knowledge of what will bring you happiness and fulfillment. That voice is very quiet, like a whisper. Over time, and mostly through the challenges in life, you will learn to hear it more clearly. Whenever you feel that tug to do something new, help someone in need, or share what you have learned, listen carefully.

We each have a chance to brighten the day of another. It can be a kind smile... a simple hello... shared inspiration... or an unexpected gesture to let someone know that their being in the world makes a difference. When good things come into your life, be inspired to brighten the day of another. Pass them on!

Families are special creations made up of people who love one another and are tied together with threads of common experience, memories, and values. You are such a special part of our family and a gift to me every day.

From the first moment I laid eyes on you, we made a connection. You have brought a love and joy to my life that only a parent could know. I watched you grow and have come to understand that our lives have been brought together for a reason. I have learned as much from you as you have from me. Thank you for your love and for sharing all that is uniquely you. The bond we have found is everlasting.

Life is a journey home. As we grow and mature and travel the unknown forests, we search, like Dorothy, for Oz — looking for wisdom, courage, and love. We meet demons and dragons and somehow overcome them all. What ordinary people call coincidence has been our guide. Finally, after great struggle, we realize we are already and always home. We snap our ruby slippers and revel in the acknowledgment that all we have needed in our lives has always been there.

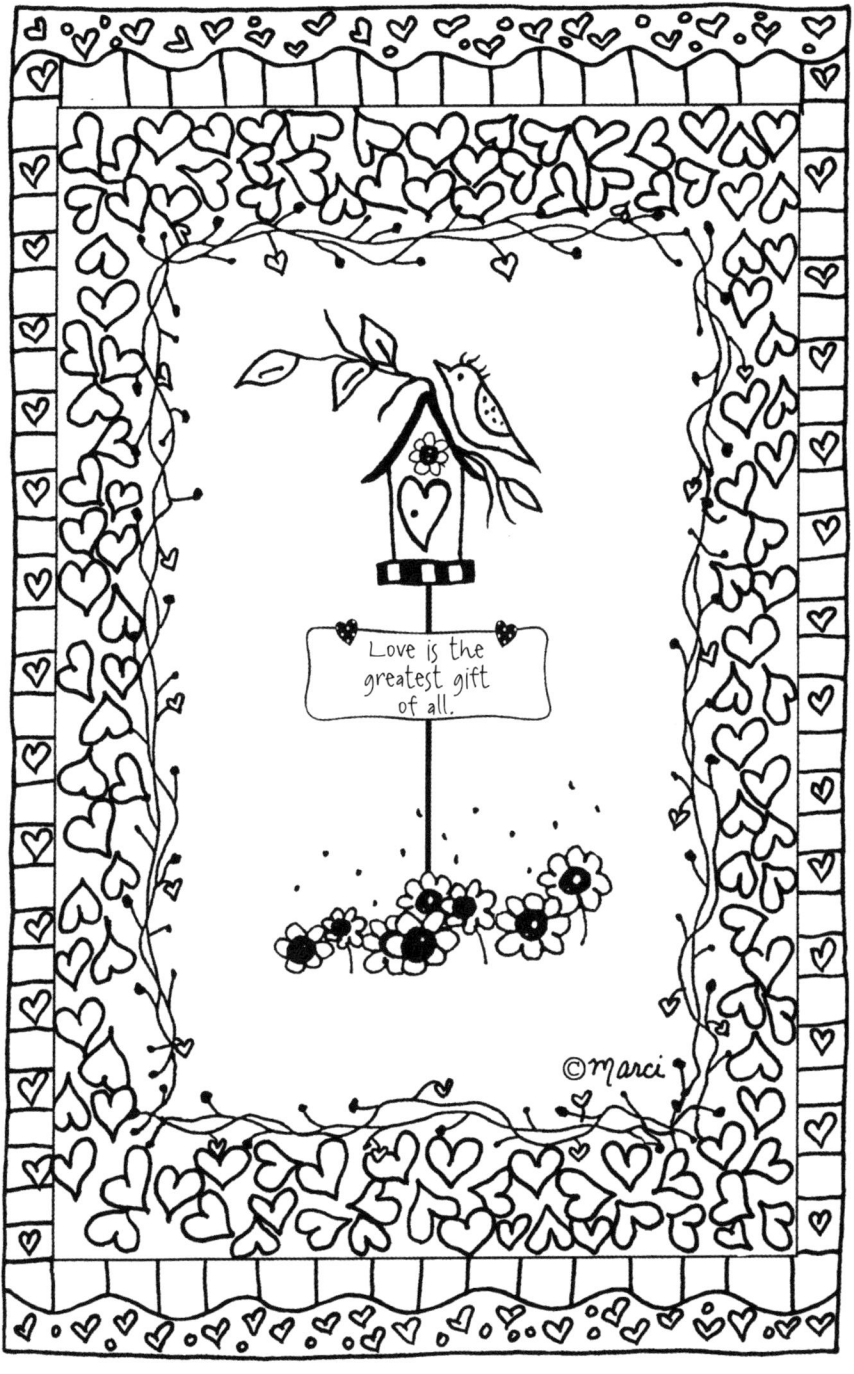

Love means accepting the love of others as they give it. This is the way to experience unconditional love.

Love means giving all you have and asking for little in return. It is sharing the joys but also supporting another through sorrow and spiritual growth.

Love means acknowledging that we always have a choice. Love is not a feeling... love is an action... love is a choice.

Love means remembering that when you're tempted to say one more thing... let it be "I love you."

Love means living in a way that demonstrates a belief in another's goodness... always positive, always encouraging, and always full of faith.

Friendship is one of life's greatest treasures, and it is a gift that lasts a lifetime. We create bonds during times in our lives when our beliefs and our experiences are shaping who we are. Those bonds cannot be broken by the passing of time, even when life gets so busy that we lose touch. Let friends know that you think of them often… and they will always have a special place in your heart.

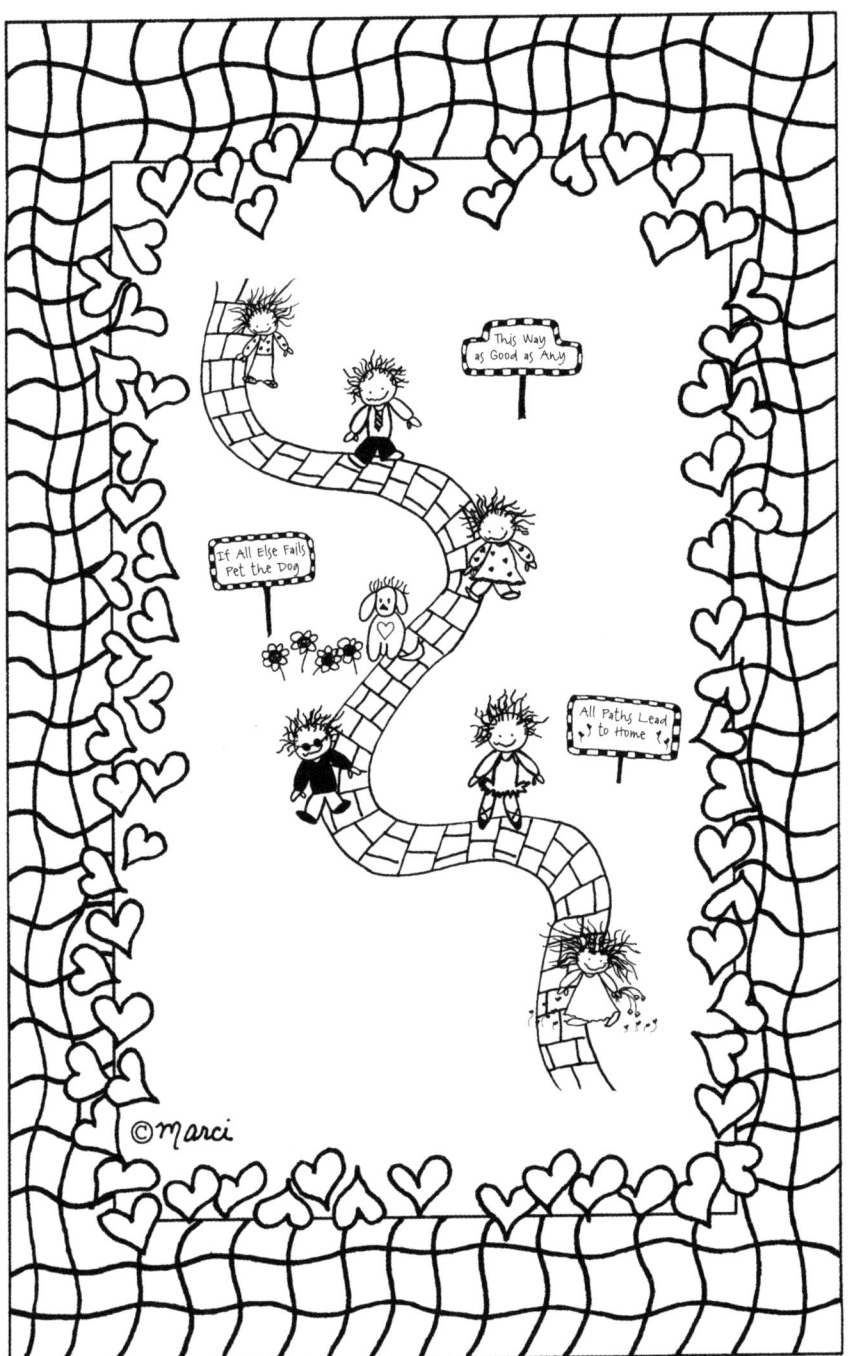

Sometimes the road of life will take you to a place you had planned... Sometimes it will show you a surprise around the bend you could never have anticipated. You must make decisions based on the information you have... accept the ups and downs as they come... and live "one day at a time." Often you will find it is only when you look back that you can see that what you had thought was a "wrong turn" has brought you to exactly the right place and that every step was a right one after all!

Keep It Simple

©marci

Believe that everything is working out for your highest good.

Live each day one at a time.

Let go of things you cannot change.

Have faith... your angel is always with you, enfolding you in God's grace.

Know that you are loved.

Be at PEACE in Your
Mind and Heart

©marci

Hold positive thoughts in your heart and be at peace...

Peace as you begin each day, always looking forward with hope and optimism.

Peace as you look back at your life, accepting that every step was for the greater good.

Peace as you sleep, knowing that your soul is in the care of the angels.

Think of Each Day as a New Start

©marci

Each day is a chance to being again, to wipe the slate clean, and to remember that today is the only day that exists. The past is gone... tomorrow is in the future... but today is a chance for a new start!

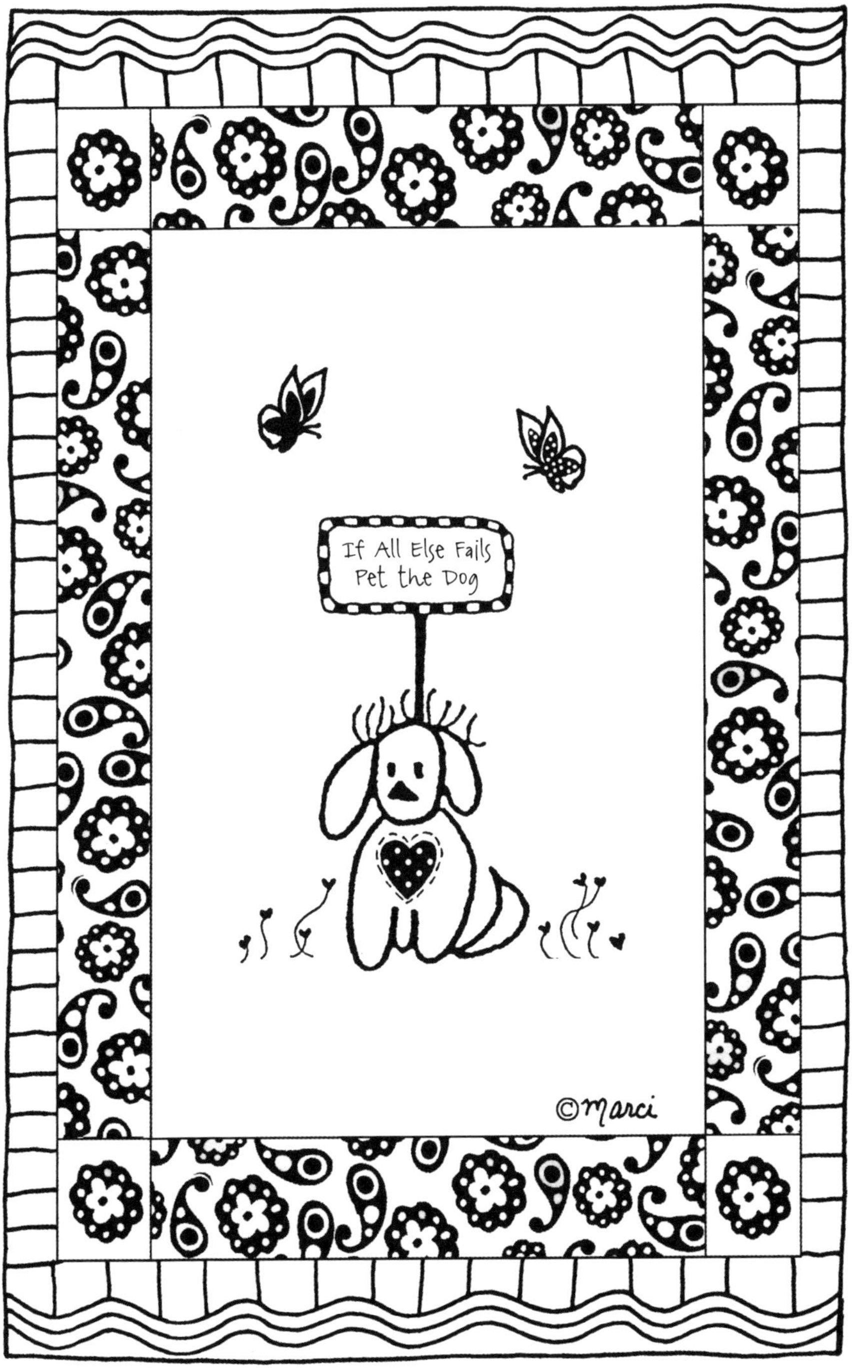
If All Else Fails
Pet the Dog
©Marci

Whatever is happening in your life, keep these things in mind…

Big problems can be solved in small steps.

When you are still, the gentle voice from within will guide you… listen carefully.

Remember to pray, and let God take the burden of worry from your heart.

Accept that we each learn life's lessons in our own way.

A lot of people love you more than words can say.

Hope is believing that miracles are possible!

©marci

Hope is a gift we can give to ourselves... When we choose this attitude and tap into our inner reserves, we are rewarded with the knowledge of what we have learned in life. The decision to look forward, stay positive, and remain hopeful is a key that unlocks the door to possibilities and, when shared, returns to renew the spirit.

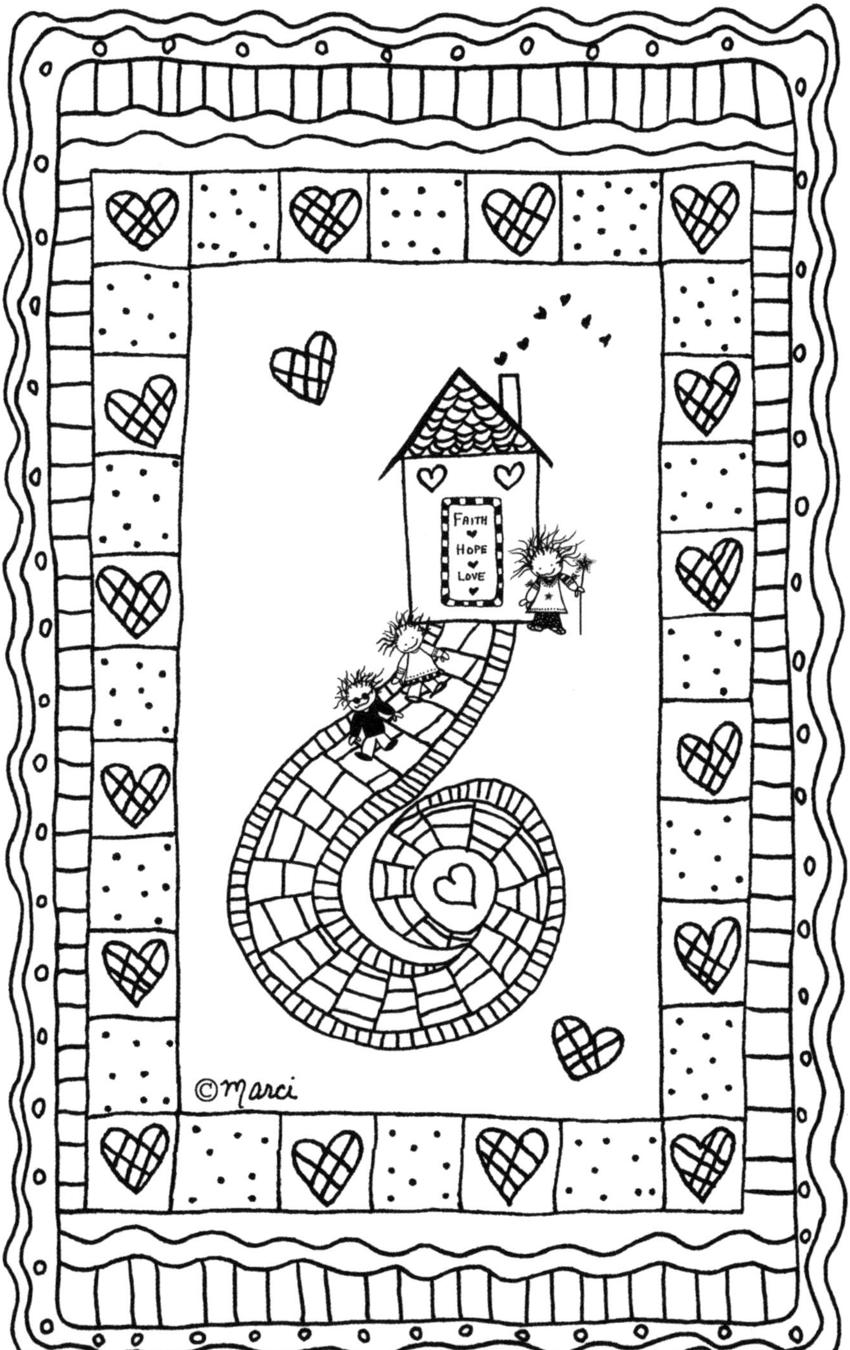
FAITH
HOPE
LOVE
©Marci

No matter where life takes you or what path you choose, you will always meet challenges. That is the way life is. There are no guarantees, and no matter how many things you do right or how many rules you follow, there will always be that fork in the road that makes you choose between this way or that. Whenever you meet this place, remember these things: You are loved... love will sustain you. You are strong... prayer will get you through anything. You are wise... the greatest gift of all lies within you.

Follow Your Dreams

Write Down Your Dream and Tuck It Away, Entrusting That All Things Will Come at the Right Time

©marci

Your life holds for you endless possibilities. You have built a solid foundation, and you have worked hard for it. Continue to do what is necessary to move forward one day at a time. Write down your dream and tuck it away — entrusting that all things will come at the right time. Keep sight always of what is important in life.

Remember that dreams are the start of every great adventure. When you close your eyes and imagine your happy and successful self in the future, you are beginning your journey!

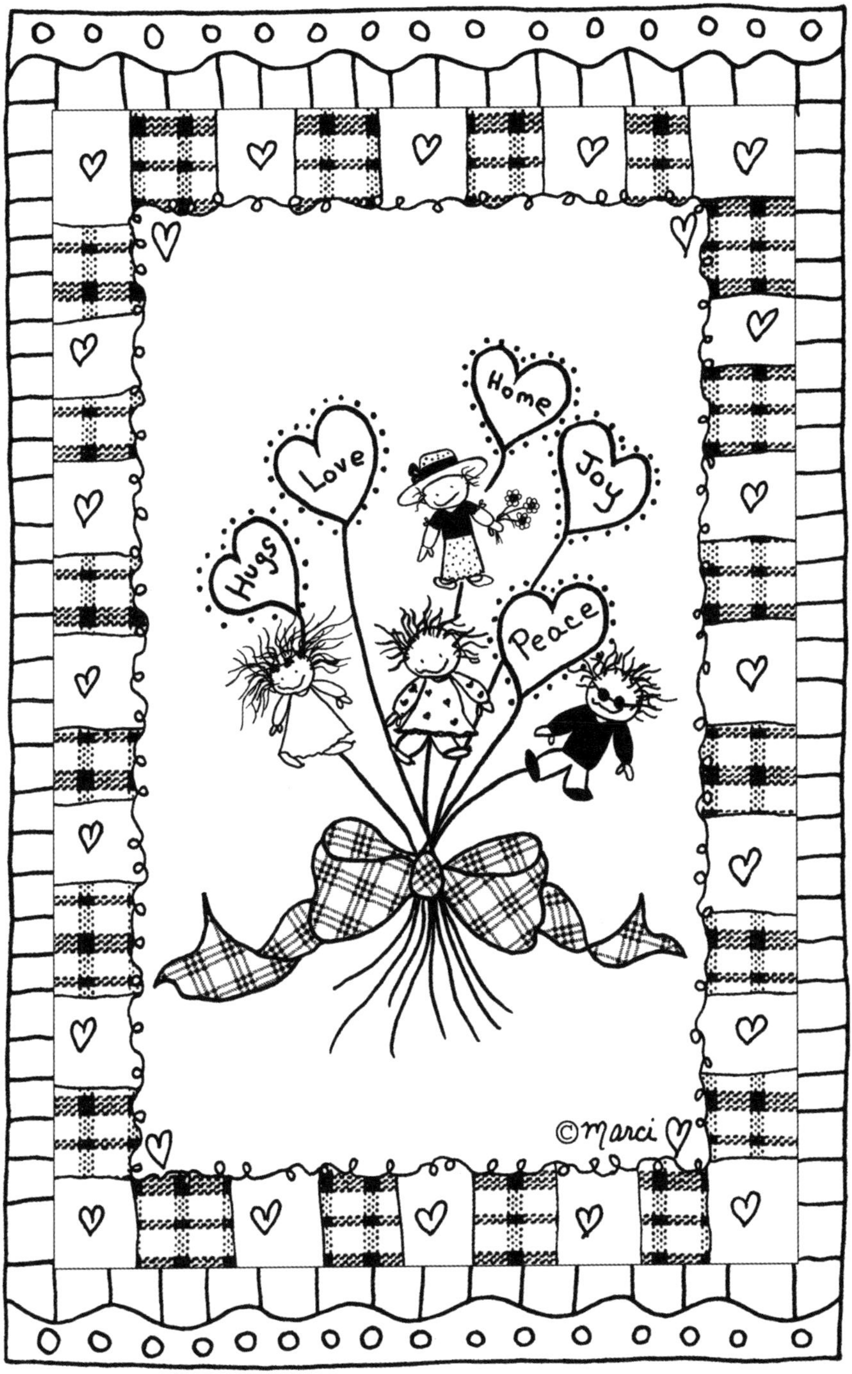
Home
Love
Joy
Hugs
Peace
©Marci

My Wishes for You

I wish you a life filled with love... a true love to share your every dream... family love to warm your heart... and priceless love found in the gift of friendship.

I wish you peace... peace in knowing who you are... peace in knowing what you believe in... and peace in the understanding of what is important in life.

I wish you joy... joy as you awaken each day with gratitude in your heart for new beginnings... joy when you surrender to the beauty of a flower or a baby's smile... and joy, a hundred times returned, for each time you've brought happiness to another's heart.

Daughter, You Are
a Gift to Me

©Marci

The day you came into my life was a beautiful day for me. Like an answered prayer, you were placed in my arms, and I knew my life had changed forever. Loving you has allowed me to experience unconditional love. Watching you pursue your dreams has given me inspiration. Sharing your happiness has taught me the meaning of joy. I am so thankful for the day that an angel blessed my life with the beautiful gift of you!

Your Love Is a Gift
and a Blessing

©marci

Some people have a way of brightening someone's day... and it's with little things that mean so much. There is a phone call at just the right time, a hug when it is needed, or a comforting word of encouragement. That special person is you!

Hope
Love
Strength
Wisdom
Love Is the Greatest
Gift of All
©Marci

May you be blessed with all the good things in life... faith, hope, love, and the blessing of good friends. If you have these things, whatever challenges life brings, you will get through. Your faith will light your path... hope will keep you strong... the love you give to others will bring you joy... and your friendships will remind you of what is important in life.

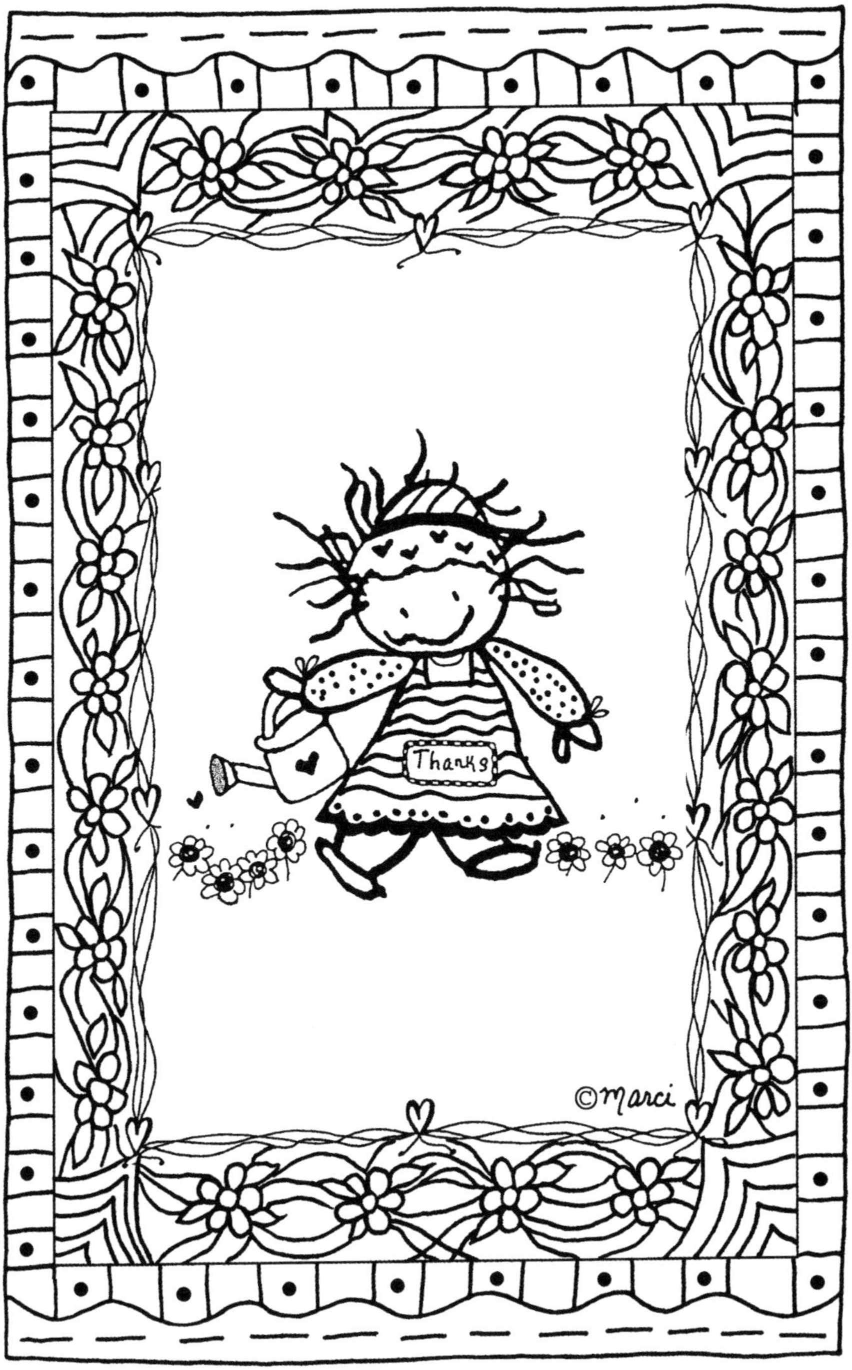
Thanks
©Marci

Daughter, your love is a blessing every day. Thank you for allowing me into your inner world to share your hopes and dreams... for teaching me as much as I have taught you... and for bringing so much love into my life.

©marci

I want you to always remember how much you mean to me. The joys we have shared and the memories we have made through our lives are a gift beyond measure. Today, consider yourself hugged!

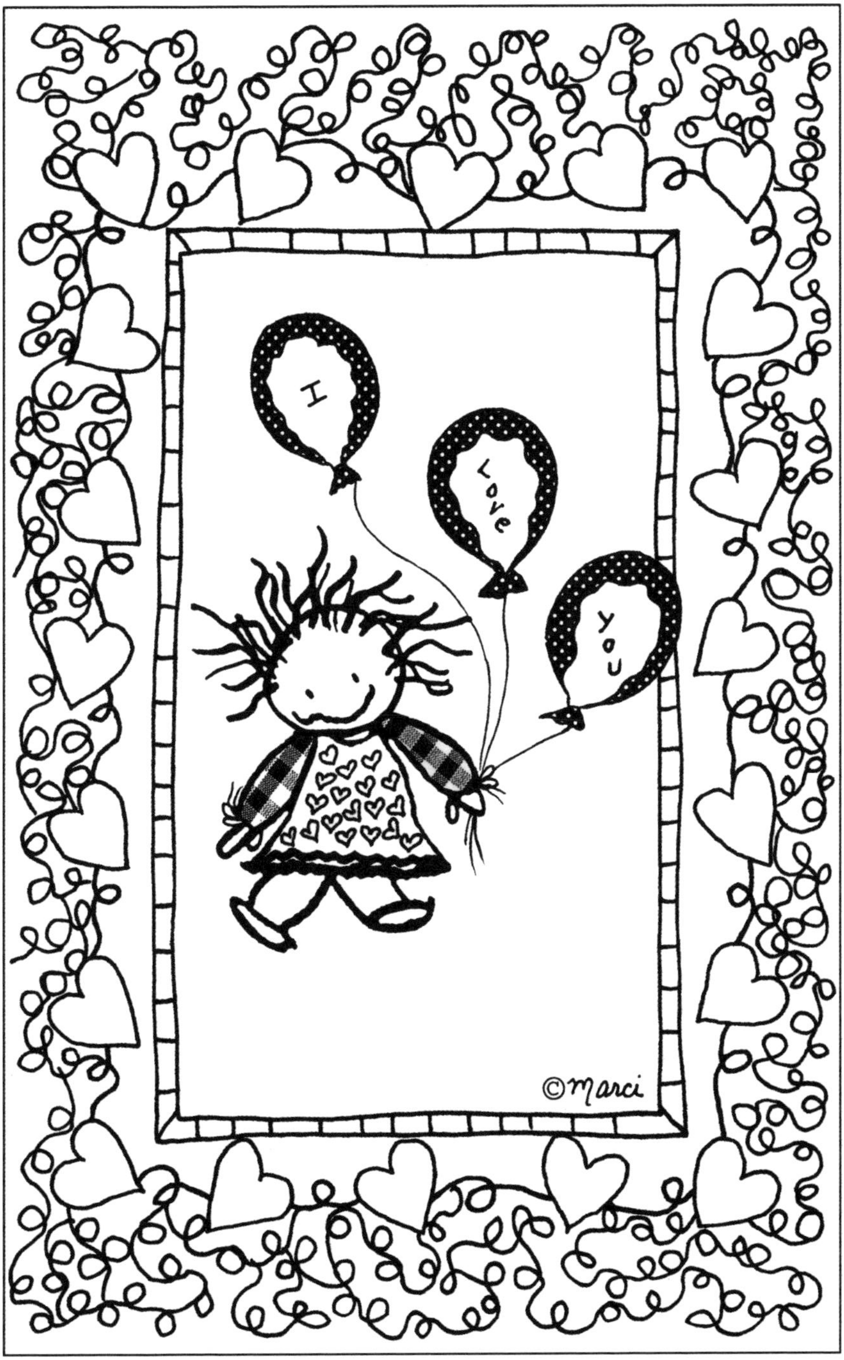
I
Love
you
©Marci

Never forget and never doubt how much you are loved. As surely as the sun rises each morning... and with the same certainty that the moon will affect the tides... know that I will always love you with all my heart.